My Exercise Diary

Written by Alison Hawes
Photographed by Steve Lumb

Collins

On Monday I went swimming.

I had fun.

Tuesday

On Tuesday I went riding.

I had fun.

On Wednesday I went skateboarding.

I had fun.

On Thursday I went climbing.

I had fun.

Friday

On Friday I went trampolining.
I had fun.

Saturday

On Saturday I went rollerblading.
I had fun.

On Sunday we went to the park.
We all had fun.

My Exercise Diary

Monday

Tuesday

Friday

Saturday

Wednesday

Thursday

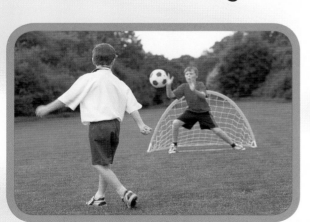

Sunday

Ideas for reading

Written by Linda Pagett B.Ed (hons), M.Ed
Lecturer and Educational Consultant

Reading objectives:
- read some common irregular words
- read and understand simple sentences
- use phonic knowledge to decode regular words and read them aloud accurately
- demonstrate understanding when talking with others about what they have read

Communication and language objectives:
- listen to stories, accurately anticipating key events and respond to what they hear with relevant comments, questions or actions
- answer "how" and "why" questions about their experiences and in response to stories
- express themselves effectively, showing awareness of listeners' needs
- give their attention to what others say and respond appropriately

Curriculum links: Physical Development; PSHE

High frequency words: on, I, went, had, to, the, all, we

Interest words: exercise, Monday, Tuesday, Wednesday, skateboarding, Thursday, Friday, trampolining, Saturday, rollerblading, Sunday

Word count: 66

Resouces: small whiteboard, pen, calendar

Build a context for reading

- Remind the children of the days of the week by showing them the calendar. Chant the days together and then take turns saying a day each in order.

- Look at the front cover and discuss the title and picture, explaining that this book is a diary. Read pp2-3 together and ask the children to predict what will happen on subsequent days.

- Walk through the book up to p13, looking at the pictures and discussing what the boy is doing on each page.

Understand and apply reading strategies

- Ask the children to read aloud and independently up to p13. Observe, prompt and praise correct one-to-one matching, re-reading to clarify meaning and using initial phonemes to identify words.

- Re-read the book again together, to practise fluency. *How does the boy feel when he takes part in these activities?*